The Story of
Prince Charles

First published in Great Britain by Colour Library Books Ltd.
© 1984 Illustrations and text: Colour Library Books Ltd.,
   Guildford, Surrey, England.
Display and text filmsetting by Acesetters Ltd.,
   Richmond, Surrey, England.
Colour separations by Llovet, Barcelona, Spain,
Printed and bound in Barcelona, Spain.
by JISA-RIEUSSET and EUROBINDER.
All rights reserved
ISBN 0 86283 173 3
COLOUR LIBRARY BOOKS

The Story of Prince Charles

Royal Heritage Series

Text by TREVOR HALL

Produced by Ted Smart and David Gibbon

Royce
PUBLICATIONS

When, shortly before his Investiture as Prince of Wales, Prince Charles was asked whether he was just a little apprehensive, he said, somewhat wryly, "As long as I don't get covered too much in egg and tomato, I'll be all right". It was a casual comment delivered without too much significance, but in a way it says a lot about the role of princes today. The real eggs and tomatoes are no great menace – several have been thrown his way in the course of his public life, along with the occasional placard or empty beer bottle, and more death threats than he cares to record. What really concerns him is that in a rapidly changing world the ancient institution of which he is both heir and future trustee should not – at least through any fault of his – be caught with egg on its face.

No better example of his dilemma presents itself than the question of his marriage. For years the issue of when, rather than whom, he would marry provided almost daily newspaper fodder and, when in his mid-twenties he said that "about thirty" seemed a good time to marry, the speculation became positively climactic. On reaching thirty he probably regretted those words more than any of the hundreds of thousands of others he had delivered in the previous decade. They put intense pressure on him to find a wife speedily while he himself knew haste was the greatest hazard. His responsibility to himself was to find a partner for life. His responsibility to his country was to provide a Princess of Wales and future Queen with impeccable credentials, no "past", and a flair for the job. It took twelve years of his adulthood to accomplish this. At the end of a long, much publicised line of girlfriends came Lady Diana Spencer – by universal agreement the biggest favour Prince Charles could have done for himself, his family, the Crown, country and Commonwealth.

On his own account he is not the least concerned at Diana's immense publicity and limitless popularity: they merely confirm his own supreme satisfaction with the obvious success of this most important venture. On more than one public occasion – and in her embarrassed presence – he has waxed lovingly about his good fortune, and in doing so has betrayed a sense of his belief that all has gone well, and of his confidence that it will continue to do so. That famous wedding-day kiss on the balcony of Buckingham Palace, unprecedented though it was, seemed the natural expression of his happiness, and in many an unguarded moment he has spontaneously taken up his wife's hand, and pressed his lips against it – a gesture not only of quaint gallantry, but the more significant for his being conscious of the accepted restraints of royal behaviour in public.

The consummation of his long quest also marks the beginning of a new chapter in Prince Charles' life – the break between a bachelor life in which he had largely followed advice and obeyed rules which he may not have originated, and an existence as a husband and parent in which decisions in balancing family and public life are ultimately his. He has left his quarters at Buckingham Palace, now taken over by Prince Andrew, and runs an independent London home and office in Kensington Palace. He discarded the public offer of Chevening House in Kent for his own country home, Highgrove House in Gloucestershire, paid for from his not insubstantial personal funds. In supporting his wife's wish to have her baby in hospital, to take him with her to Australia, to invite the Press to Kensington Palace to take pictures of the growing Prince William, Charles is not breaking old-established rules for their own sake, but rather emphasising that traditions should know their place. The monarchy, like everything else, must keep on the move.

Perhaps marriage, and the independence from elders which it brings, has proved the catalyst. Prince Charles was brought up in arguably the most unenviable circumstances – a conservative post-war era, a conservative household, a circle of conservative friends and acquaintants. It was not easy for his parents to go trend-setting in the business of bringing up their son, but Prince Philip was almost certainly insistent that the plunge should, where possible, be taken. Charles became the first heir apparent to be educated outside the Palace walls, and if there is any truth in the story that he once asked the Queen, "Mummy, what *are* schoolboys?" he found out when he went to Hill House School in Knightsbridge, shortly after his eighth birthday. There were 120 of them there, and for the first time he had to mix with the sons of middle-class and foreign families.

The process was far from easy, and the confidence that Prince Charles says his public school education gave him showed little sign of blossoming until he was well into the secondary stage. Any initial progress was blighted by his untimely creation as Prince of Wales in 1958, at the end of his first year at Cheam School. The Queen's public announcement of the grant of the title was televised live, watched by an unsuspecting Prince Charles, and a group of his school-friends in his headmaster's study. "I remember being acutely embarrassed", he said. "All the others turned to me in amazement."

It was Gordonstoun, selected on the strength of Prince Philip's personal experience as much as for its geographical remoteness, to which Charles was sent early in 1962, which really brought him out. He owes his will power, self-control, endurance and methodical approach to all he undertakes, to the all-round educational concept on which the school was founded. Above all, it offered an adventurous interlude in his hitherto sheltered life – the school ran its own fire brigade, sea and mountain rescue operations, life-saving and coastguard services – "and we were damn good."

It was here that the famous cherry brandy incident first initiated him into the wonders of newspaper dramatisation. It was here that his taste for amateur dramatics developed and his love of flying was kindled. And it was from here that he profited so well from an exchange scheme which took him to Australia for a six-month secondment to Timbertop School near Geelong. This proved a stimulating, eye-opening time, and one which imbued him with a fascination for Australia and a respect for her people which has grown with every subsequent visit. His experience effectively rendered Timbertop a sort of finishing school. His shyness completely disappeared: "Australia cured me of that", he admitted. His detective confirmed the transition: "I went out there with a boy", he said, "and returned with a man".

He was by no means the first member of the Royal Family to go to university, and he is pleased he did. When his father once confessed himself unaffected by not having gone to university, Prince Charles parried almost immediately, "I am one of those stupid bums who did go to university – and I think its helped me". At least Trinity College, Cambridge allowed him to indulge what he has called his "overdeveloped sense of history" in a three-year degree course which included archaeology and anthropology. He was also able to expand his passion for music. He had tried the trumpet at prep school, but gave up because his teacher couldn't stand the noise, so at college he took up the 'cello and persevered for several years. Unfortunately, events have overtaken him: his time became more limited and his 'cello – once famous for having snapped a string in the face of Prince Edward during the filming of *Royal Family* – languished unattended for years before recently being sold in support of the Royal Opera House Development Appeal.

His penchant for acting matured while at Cambridge, and he diversified from revue to club drama, finding himself on the receiving end of custard pies or sitting in dustbins in the quest for making people laugh. Goonery – one of his favourite childhood entertainments – has always held a private fascination for him, and both as an amateur actor and as a Prince on duty he has given it full rein. He turned up at a Master Tailors' dinner dressed in hacking jacket and Garter Star one evening, after hearing that the magazine *Tailor and Cutter* had voted him the worst dressed man of the year. He sportingly took part in a camel race at an Olympia horse show, dressed in polo strip, mounting by means of a decorator's ladder, and complaining afterwards of the pungent smell "from both ends" of the animal.

During his time at Cambridge, he was ceremonially invested as Prince of Wales at Caernarvon Castle. Unlike his immediate predecessor, the future Edward VIII, he did not jib at the prospect of taking part in a modern version of an artificially-revived medieval ritual, and throwing himself into the spirit and detail of the occasion included spending a term at the University of Wales to learn Welsh, as well as about the Welsh. By the time of the ceremony, at the beginning of July 1969, he was bilingual – a fact as much appreciated by his subjects as his charm and modesty – and he has invariably used Welsh as well as English during his subsequent visits to the principality. These nowadays take place at the rate of approximately a dozen a year.

In a way the Investiture, and the four-day tour of Wales which followed it, marked the beginning of his life of public service. He had undertaken occasional duties already, though his final year at Trinity College prevented him from carrying out anything like a full schedule of engagements, but somehow this colourful and much publicised event launched him into what King George VI called "the firm" and Queen Mary called "the trade". Within the year he was on an official visit to Canada, having already toured Australia and New Zealand, and visited Japan, Malta and Strasbourg in a public capacity. Within a further eight months he had visited eight more countries officially, including Fiji whose independence celebrations he attended in October 1970. He had by then taken his seat in the House of Lords, obtained his grade A pilot's licence and – as a prelude to six years of voluntary service in the forces – begun to train at the RAF College at Cranwell.

He had decided to follow his time with the RAF by a commission in the Navy. It would, he said, "stand me in good stead for the rest of my life". Cranwell taught him, among other things, how to parachute – "It's easy when you're pushed", he joked, years later – and he was awarded his wings in 1971. That year he began his five years in the Navy, serving on guided missile destroyers, frigates and the minesweeper *HMS Bronington,* which was his first and only command. Part of his continuing training involved a Royal Marines assault course – "a most horrifying expedition" – and a solo flying programme from which he emerged as the best officer of his course. When he quit the Navy in 1976 he was better qualified and much more experienced than any Prince of Wales completing service in the armed forces of his time.

In the five years between then and his marriage, he became a highly travelled member of the Royal Family, proving himself a much sought-after guest of foreign, and particularly Commonwealth, countries, and a personable and popular roving ambassador. He had already been much commended for his roving eye for the ladies too, and even by then had been married off several times in the imagination of numerous rumour-mongers. This inevitable consequence of being seen in female company at polo matches, theatres and game fairs, or of having invited girls to Balmoral, Sandringham or Windsor, riled him. "I have only met the girl once", he complained after a rather formal introduction to Princess Caroline of Monaco, "and they are already trying to marry us off." It wasn't the first, or last time. Hot on the heels of the State Visit to Britain of the Grand Duke of Luxembourg came the news that his elder daughter Princess Marie-Astrid was on the brink of becoming the next Princess of Wales. The fact that she was a Roman Catholic, far from discouraging speculation, merely fuelled talk of constitutional changes to accommodate the forthcoming marriage, and even the Queen's meeting with the Pope in 1980 was rumoured to have embraced this delicate subject.

If Prince Charles knew that religious considerations made such a union impossible he was also aware that his position obliged him to allow other friendships to fade for a variety of different reasons. Before he was twenty he acknowledged the advantage of choosing a wife who would readily appreciate what marriage into the Royal Family would involve and demand – "a way of life, a job, a life in which she's got a contribution to make" – and many of his girlfriends clearly failed to meet that standard. Discretion was a major requirement, and public utterances on the subject by such as Jane Ward and Lady Sarah Spencer ruled them out with frightening immediacy. Ability to stand the strain of publicity was another: "It tends to put the really nice ones off", he admitted ruefully as early as 1972. Chastity was yet another, and, whether jilted or jealous, the revelations of former boyfriends of the Prince's female companions frequently ensured the premature withering of royal friendships. Stability was perhaps the most important demand, and one which Prince Charles has always made clear. "My marriage", he once said, "has to be for ever. The whole point about the marriage contract was that it was for life."

Few people really expected Lady Diana Spencer to live up to all of those rigorous demands. Barely nineteen when both she and Prince Charles were first spotted by lurking Press cameras at Balmoral, she seemed just too young, too naive, too "nice" to take on what the Prince had already described as a "hideously complicated" enterprise. She soon showed what she was made of, however, dealing quietly and competently with the world's Press as, for three long months of mounting speculation, it trailed her relentlessly from her Knightsbridge flat to the Pimlico kindergarten where she worked. When the Balmoral visit was followed by an invitation to Sandringham to celebrate Prince Charles' 32nd birthday, popular conclusions were all but drawn. But Charles went on a trip to India and Nepal a fortnight later, during which he is said to have confessed, "I am terrified of getting it wrong", and when he finally decided to pop the question, he held off her ready agreement, insisting that she should not give him her answer before due consideration away from the pressures of London. She went to Australia to visit her mother and stepfather, and came back as firmly convinced as ever. His amazement was exceeded only by his obvious delight.

A spectator relying on outward appearances would not readily recognise much of a change in Prince Charles since that monumental wedding in July 1981, the format and content of which he did much to mastermind. There is in his demeanour a certain glow of satisfaction, perhaps of fulfilment now that he has provided his future subjects with not only an immensely popular Princess of Wales but also a delightful and healthy second heir to the throne. But "the firm" continues to exhaust a huge amount of his public time, and he has not let up in lending his assistance to worthy causes.

In this respect, he has tended to deviate from the traditional support lent by royalty, and has taken several unexpected turns in the distribution of his time and largesse. The task of raising the *Mary Rose* owed much of its financial support and respectability with the public to almost three years in which his interest verged on the fanatical and prompted him to complete no fewer than ten dives to inspect the submerged wreck. His chairmanship of The Prince's Trust may seem respectably titular, but he goes rather more deeply into its work and insists on actually meeting the unfortunate people who have had to battle away very much on their own to lift themselves above the squalour and despair of their surroundings. Photographs of British princes handing over cheques to enable an unemployed group to start a fish-and-chip shop begin with him. It evidences a very wealthy man's awareness of the effects of social decline as well as his determination to give the lead to alleviate it. More recently, he caused more raised eyebrows when he consented to become Patron of the Royal College of Psychiatrists: even Buckingham Palace admitted being very interested in how that particular association would flourish.

Since mid-1983 he has felt much freer – now that his wife has so admirably proved her ability to undertake solo engagements – to follow his own programme of duties, and his public life is gradually resuming the character of his bachelor days. But the appearance of continuity is deceptive. His marriage, like most, has involved changes that perhaps even he did not envisage. Several firm friends of his early days – though discretion dictated that there should always be few – found themselves surplus to requirements, while staff at the Prince of Wales' Office – including personal detectives and valets – were dispensed with at alarming speed. His wife has been named as the force behind these changes, as indeed with forcing Charles' brief and none-too-successful venture into horseracing to an abrupt end. Endless rumours, within only months of their wedding, of her antipathy to stag-hunting, pheasant-shooting, and the traditional pleasures of the landed gentry – including polo – paved the way for an anticipated break-up of the marriage. Those in search of scandal were, of course, ultimately disappointed: if there were any difficulties, the marriage had already proved sufficiently sound to withstand them. It subsequently withstood another barrage of speculation when, in the aftermath of Prince William's birth, Diana's apparent obsession with the need to lose weight rekindled talk of disunity within the family to the point where one gossip columnist branded her "a monster:

a fiend" who "is making Charles desperately unhappy".

Whatever the truth behind those uncomfortable spells, it is unthinkable that Prince Charles was ever other than the kind, understanding and considerate husband everyone thought he would be. His open display of affection for his wife – from that first engagement-day photocall to the playful hugs that punctuate an afternoon's visit to Smith's Lawn – make his infatuation clear for all to see. His praise of her is no less overt. On the day her pregnancy was announced, he called her "my dear wife, who has such a wonderful effect on everyone". In Australia he described himself as "lucky enough to have married her", and during a speech after a polo match he made a point of thanking "my wife for her support in coming to see her husband make a fool of himself".

Parenthood has provided him with one of the few thrills still otherwise remaining beyond his personal experience. He threw himself into the prospect of fatherhood as vigorously as he has espoused any new venture. He read an endless supply of books on pregnancy and baby-care, almost to the point where Diana publicly – though tolerantly – deplored his constant advice and interference. Like few, if any, royal fathers since Prince Albert, he attended his son's birth, and soon became besotted with him. He bathed him whenever the opportunity arose, was seen carrying him on and off aircraft, and has continually regaled the public with details of the baby's habits – including the less desirable ones – with evident relish. Needless to say, the young Prince William was rarely left out of any speech his father made during the three major tours in 1983. How different from his great-grandfather, George V, who was reputed to have justified his disciplinarian treatment of his sons by the belief that princes should be brought up to fear their fathers: "I was always frightened of my father: they must be frightened of me".

Prince Charles is, of course, well suited to family life. Now, as in his youth, it furnishes a haven from the pressures of his position, and provides the only real guarantee of discretion and privacy in a life of fierce and remorseless publicity. The cynic would probably dismiss as only natural his respect for the family unit – after all he does have something of a vested interest in maintaining both it and its relevance to the hereditary system of monarchy to which he is heir.

When he does succeed to the throne, however, it will be in a completely different atmosphere from the veneration which surrounded his mother's accession in 1952. The unquestioning acceptance of standards and examples from above has already vanished in the breezier, debunking social climate of the last two decades. The Establishment is no longer unassailable: the monarchy above all has to justify its existence now, and will continue to have to do so. In that light it seems unavoidable that the institution will have to depend for its reputation more and more on personalities rather than on tradition and the notion of continuity.

"We are a family of human beings, not a set of symbols", Prince Charles once said. "I think everybody would want us to be real." Though he almost invariably refers to his mother as "The Queen", he pays tribute to her motherly warmth and wisdom – "a marvellous person and a wonderful mother", he calls her. He generously acknowledges Prince Philip's enormous influence – introducing new experiences, curbing immoderate ambitions, encouraging a love of the great outdoors. He has always been full of admiration for his grandmother, Queen Elizabeth the Queen Mother, whom he described as "the most wonderful example of fun, laughter, warmth, infinite security and, above all, exquisite taste in so many things". His praise for his great-uncle, Lord Mountbatten, borders on the reverential.

Indeed, he has a respectful, even adoring, attitude to most of his royal forebears – including the much-maligned George III whose reputation he has done much to restore, and the exiled Edward VIII whom Prince Charles visited during his last years. In a way, this ready deference to people who were not only his ancestors but also his predecessors is an indispensable requirement of the job he will one day take over. In the chillingly realistic world of today, you certainly need to believe wholeheartedly in an institution like the monarchy, which is not without its illogicality and appeals very much more to the heart than to the head. Prince Charles has that inborn and matured conviction, and it could well make him one of Britain's best constitutional monarchs when the time comes.

So surging has his popularity been in the last decade that he has frequently been considered ready for the throne no matter how soon it should become vacant and, for that reason, the question of the Queen's abdication has been much discussed. The idea has its attractions, and the possibility can never be irrevocably discarded. But what purpose would it serve? The Queen is clearly happy to continue being Queen, and is competent to do so. Prince Charles is thus left free to follow his own line – both public and private – unhampered by the ubiquitous demands of protocol and diplomacy in everything he does and says. Neither mother nor son seems to relish the idea of setting a precedent for a morally compulsory retirement procedure in the monarchical system – otherwise we are condemned to an endless run of 35-year reigns presided over by perpetually middle-aged sovereigns. There is no charm in that prospect: none of the luck-of-the-draw mentality which can put a monarch on the throne unexpectedly young and fresh, or keep one there well into wise old age.

Prince Charles seems content enough to bide his time. Come the day when the comparatively cosmopolitan life of a Prince of Wales must be exchanged for the appalling restrictions of a Head of State, he will doubtless be glad he did.

The fame surrounding Prince Charles' birth dogged him throughout childhood but the family provided some respite. Besides his parents (top left, early in 1949), he just remembers his grandfather, George VI, and great grandmother, Queen Mary; both attended his christening in 1948 (top centre). A sister, Anne, arrived in 1950: (centre left) the family at Clarence House in 1951 and (above) at Windsor in 1959. Lord Mountbatten – seen (above left) with his wife, Charles and Anne in 1954 – became Charles' "honorary grandfather". For the Queen Mother, "whose touch", Charles once said, "can turn everything to gold", two dutiful grandchildren brought baby Prince Andrew to Clarence House on her 60th birthday (top). Even after Charles' Investiture in 1969 (right) marked the beginning of his public life, the family remained as close knit as ever: (left) at Balmoral in 1979. Charles attended the State Opening of Parliament for the first time in 1967 (overleaf).

Balmoral Castle, where the three royal brothers were photographed with the Queen and Prince Philip to mark their 32nd wedding anniversary (top left), has a special place in Prince Charles' affections, and it was here that he decided to have his 30th birthday photographs taken in 1978. In some, his Scottish affections are betrayed and he wears the Hunting Stewart tartan kilt which once belonged to George VI. With him is his golden Labrador, Harvey. (Above) Charles at Ascot, in the days when the Royal Family used to gather for a morning canter down the course. (Opposite) Like father, like son. Prince Philip sees Charles gain his wings at RAF Cranwell in 1971.

(Above right and opposite page) Charles enjoying Brazilian festivities in Rio in 1978 and (above, centre) putting in a more formal appearance after the dancing. Business with pleasure again – and a questionable pointing of fingers – as Charles met performers at his 31st birthday concert at Wembley (top right) and singer Grace Kennedy at 1980's Royal Variety Performance (far right). Like his father, Charles regularly supported Cowes Week – sailing, wind surfing and attending formal dinners like this one (above, far right) with Lord Mountbatten in 1975. Six years later he introduced his fiancée to the public at Goldsmiths Hall, London (above and right), for a recital attended by Princess Grace of Monaco (top).

Versatility is Prince Charles' hallmark: he is equally at home on parade ground and polo field. One of his earliest ceremonial duties was at Windsor, escorting the Queen Mother at the 1969 Garter ceremony (right). He enjoys his connections with the services which taught him to fly helicopters (left, at Yeovilton in 1974) and to parachute (above right, at South Cerney in 1978), and relishes the ceremonial display of Trooping the Colour. In 1981 he was in the procession (opposite page) which was disrupted when the Queen was fired at. He was the first to assure her that the assailant had been seized. (Below) the Royal Family on the Palace balcony after that ceremony. Of all his many leisure interests, polo has remained the strongest: (above) feeding his ponies after a match at Windsor in 1979.

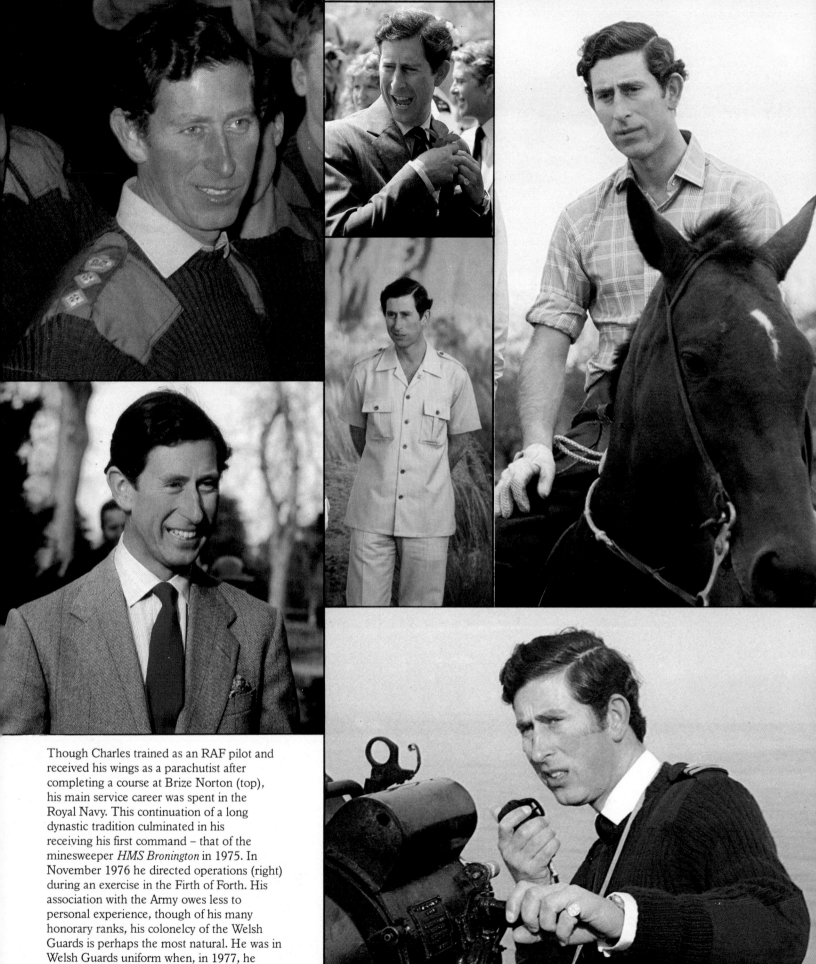

Though Charles trained as an RAF pilot and received his wings as a parachutist after completing a course at Brize Norton (top), his main service career was spent in the Royal Navy. This continuation of a long dynastic tradition culminated in his receiving his first command – that of the minesweeper *HMS Bronington* in 1975. In November 1976 he directed operations (right) during an exercise in the Firth of Forth. His association with the Army owes less to personal experience, though of his many honorary ranks, his colonelcy of the Welsh Guards is perhaps the most natural. He was in Welsh Guards uniform when, in 1977, he attended the Queen's Silver Jubilee Thanksgiving Service in St Paul's Cathedral. Behind him on that occasion (opposite page, bottom right) was the Duke of Beaufort, then Master of the Queen's Horse, a kinsman of the Royal Family whose weekly hunts in Gloucestershire Charles frequently attended.

Prince Charles' affable temperament lends a special quality to even the most mundane of engagements. He was only a few miles from his Highgrove home when, in March 1982, he visited Westonbirt Arboretum where he planted an ash sapling to commemorate his wedding (opposite page, bottom left). He rarely goes out wearing a buttonhole, because he is almost inevitably given one in the course of the day: hence the daffodil (below) during a visit to Tondu Nature Reserve in South Wales in April 1982, and the rose (opposite page, top centre) at Capital Radio's venture day in Battersea Park that June. (Bottom) a visit with Lady Diana to Broadlands to open the Mountbatten exhibition in March 1981; then to Newcastle four months afterwards (right) when he was unaccompanied by her despite the fact that it was her 20th birthday. Sometimes, of course, it's pleasant merely to relax during the hectic schedules of overseas tours: (left) while visiting America in 1977, Prince Charles rode horseback around the Texas ranch belonging to the family of a former US ambassador to Britain; (opposite page, centre) a thoughtful moment while sightseeing at Ayers Rock with the Princess of Wales at the beginning of their month-long tour of Australia in March 1983.

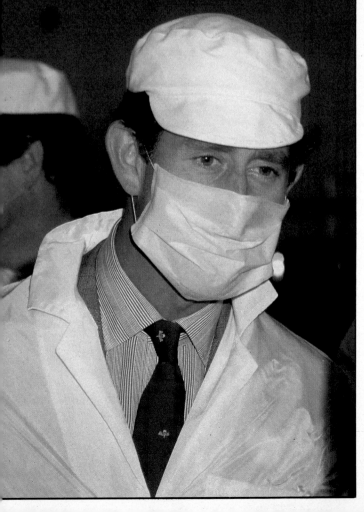

As Prince of Wales, Charles visits his principality, on average, once a month. In April 1982 he visited a Carmarthen community centre (top left) as part of a full day's work in South Wales, and that June toured a high technology plant at Brynmawr (far left) during a day in southWest Wales. As Duke of Cornwall, he pays both official and private working visits to the Duchy, and two months before the birth of Prince William, took his wife to the Scilly Isles (left) for a four-day holiday.

1980 was a busy year for the Royal Family, with the national celebration of the Queen Mother's 80th birthday in mid-July. Family festivities took place on her birthday proper – 4th August – and Charles was at Clarence House that morning (opposite page, centre right) with Prince Edward and Princess Margaret. That November he went to India where his schedule included a visit to a Sikh shrine in New Delhi, (top left), and a meeting with Mother Teresa at her Calcutta mission (left). Then, as now, the Prince both watched and played polo regularly: in July 1980, he was joined by Prince Andrew at Windsor (opposite page, top right); in August 1982 he went alone to Cowdray Park (below).

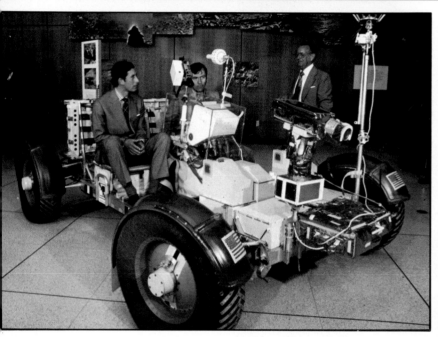

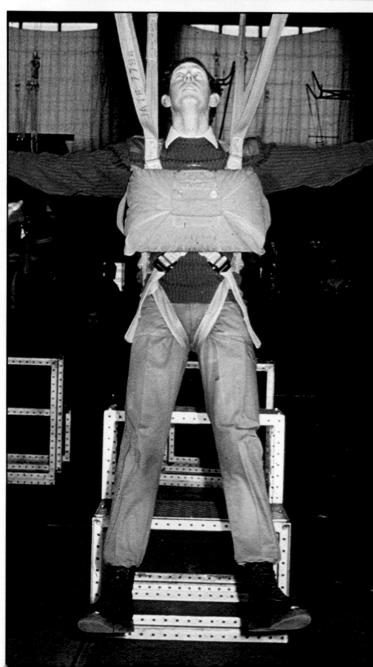

Sometimes Prince Charles finds himself in some pretty unusual situations, though fortunately most are by desire, and can be coped with, rather than by accident. His rigorous parachute training at Brize Norton in 1978 (right) probably saved him from disaster when, during the real thing, his legs became tangled in the rigging lines. A few minutes inside a moon buggy (above) during a visit to San Antonio, Texas in 1977, gave him an idea – if a slender one – of how the astronauts drove around the moon's surface several years before. That camel riding is not his *forte* was proved by the strange combination of riding hat, polo shirt, jodhpurs and decorator's ladder used to accomplish his first such experience during the Horse of the Year Show in December 1979 (top right). A whole age distant from the luxurious Royal Yacht was the simple craft (top) in which Prince Charles was punted around the marshes of a bird sanctuary in India in November 1980. Immediately behind him in the boat is his personal detective, John Maclean, who has been his bodyguard for over 15 years. (Left) a more familiar situation for Prince Charles – astride his pony shortly before a polo match at Windsor in May 1983. And a blunt reminder to brother Andrew to respect his elders and – in this game at least – betters!

A contrast in moods as Prince Charles took command of *HMS Bronington* during exercises off Scotland in November 1976. Prince Andrew, on leave from Gordonstoun School, joined him for the day (top left). (Above) a confident Prince Charles reflected on the success of the exercise. (Left) the celebrated rapport between the Prince and his grandmother was well in evidence as he accompanied her to the Thanksgiving Service for her 80th birthday in London in July 1980. "She belongs to that priceless brand of human beings", he wrote, "whose greatest gift is to enhance life for others through her own effervescent enthusiasm for life". At that time, another lady entered Prince Charles' life, and following their engagement in February 1981, they were frequently seen together in public. Their appearances that summer included visits to Royal Ascot (bottom left) and attendance at the marriage of Prince Charles' friend Nicholas Soames to Miss Catherine Weatherall at Westminster (opposite page). The Queen Mother and Princess Margaret were also in the congregation. (Below) bachelor days: Prince Charles visited the factory of Lansing Ltd at Basingstoke in October 1980.

Fun at Broadlands (left, below and right). Both Prince Charles and Lady Diana planted trees marking their visit in May 1981 to open the permanent Mountbatten exhibition.

Engagement day at Buckingham Palace. On 24th February 1981, the news all Britain had been expecting for months broke officially and Prince Charles posed (above and left) for official photographs with his 19-year-old fiancée. Lady Diana Spencer, a childhood friend, sister of one of Prince Charles' previous girlfriends, and a close companion in more recent months, looked uncannily confident as the cameras clicked. She had no doubts, she said, about the wisdom of her choice. Few really credited that at such a tender age she would stay the course. Only those few were right: she quickly became the darling of the nation and the envy of the world.

Everyone has an enduring memory of 29th July 1981 – Charles and Diana's wedding day. Prince Charles wanted the ceremony at St Paul's to be a great musical and emotional experience. So it was – but a kiss on the balcony and balloons on their going-away carriage kept it all very human.

After a fortnight's Mediterranean cruise in *Britannia,* the royal honeymooners came home to Balmoral. These pictures were taken at the Brig o' Dee on the royal estate in mid-August, at the beginning of a two-month holiday before a monumental three-day tour of Wales.

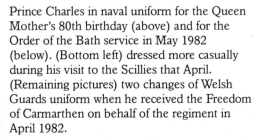

Prince Charles in naval uniform for the Queen Mother's 80th birthday (above) and for the Order of the Bath service in May 1982 (below). (Bottom left) dressed more casually during his visit to the Scillies that April. (Remaining pictures) two changes of Welsh Guards uniform when he received the Freedom of Carmarthen on behalf of the regiment in April 1982.

Charles' first steeplechase, in March 1980 (bottom right), began a short, undistinguished horseracing career, but he joined the successful House of Lords team against the Commons in a rifle shooting match at Bisley that July (right). His passion for hunting – (left) with the Quorn, December 1982 – persists. His interest in babies, evidenced by this brief encounter in Glamorgan in April 1982 (far right, centre) no doubt owed its spontaneity to the impending birth of his own son, which he attended (top right) that June. (Above and top centre) Prince Charles visiting Tresco that April. (Below) with schoolboys in Caernarvon the same month. (Right) visiting the British Steel Corporation workshops at Port Talbot in May.

With a polo handicap of 4, Prince Charles is a useful team player. He is a regular member of two national teams – Maple Leaf and the Blue Devils (below). He owes much of his success to his coach, Sinclair Hill (left); reputedly the only man who can get away with swearing at him. The Queen's presence at several of his matches – (opposite page, bottom left) at the Mountbatten Cup match in June 1982 – ensures the maximum public interest.

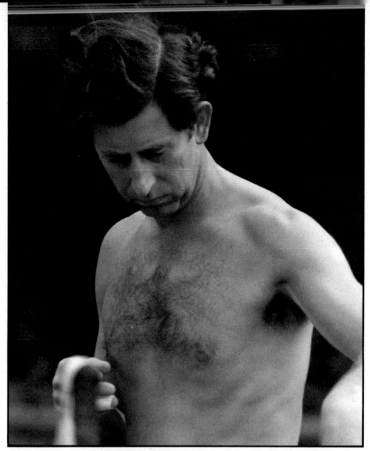

Like his father, sister and brother-in-law, Charles has taken part in the Royal Windsor Horse Show: in 1979 he competed (below) in the triathlon event. When he turned to National Hunt racing, his second placing on Long Wharf at Plumpton (below right) proved to be his best: he was unsuccessful at Cheltenham in 1981 (left), then fell from Good Prospect at Sandown (above left). By contrast, his twenty years at polo – (above right) at Windsor Great Park in July 1979 – have brought consistent rewards, including the Towry Law Cup at Windsor in his first 1982 match (opposite). His wife is a recent convert. After seeming indifferent while he played at Windsor in May 1982 (top), she publicly denied being bored when he played there a week later (right). Indeed, she was with him at Windsor again only four days before Prince William's birth (below left).

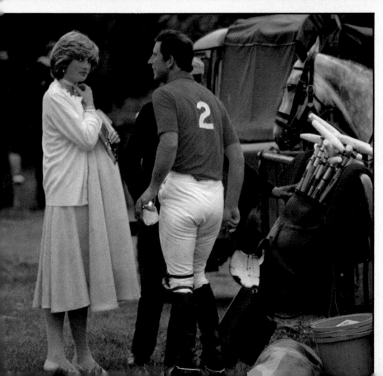

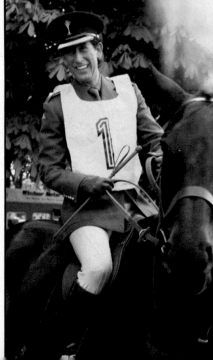

Charles piloted his own helicopter aboard the *SS Canberra* (below) to meet returning Falklands officers (top right) and men (opposite page, bottom left) at Southampton in June 1982. In July, he attended the revue *Salute to the Task Force* in London (right, above right, bottom, and opposite page, bottom centre), which began a highly successful national appeal.

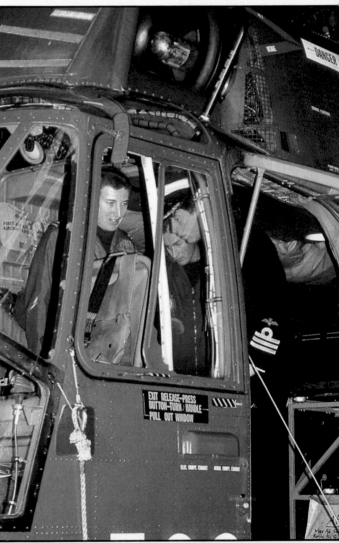

A selection of Prince Charles' engagements over twelve months, evidencing his long association with the Royal Navy. Attendance at the annual Festival of Remembrance – (far left) in November 1982 – is a "civvies" affair but uniforms mark the solemnity of the Remembrance Day Service (below centre). He always lays his own wreath, and in 1983 represented the Queen during her absence abroad. Uniforms, too, for the annual meeting and service of the Court of Trinity House in the City of London (right and far right) and for a visit to *HMS Osprey* (below, below left and bottom right).

(Previous pages) Charles with Diana at St Mary's, Scilly Isles in April 1982, and returning from Eleuthera the previous February. The birth of Prince William seemed to seal their happiness. Diana even dropped in on her way from Royal Ascot to watch Charles play polo (these pages), less than a week before her confinement.

Prince William's birth was accomplished with the minimum of fuss. Charles and Diana arrived at St Mary's Hospital in the early hours of the morning, unwitnessed by a single photographer. After a long labour and twelve hours wait by huge crowds outside, the hoped-for son was born. It was 9.03 pm on Monday, 21st June, 1982. Charles saw the birth, and said it was a bit of a shock to his system. Diana seemed none the worse as all three left to go home on the following day. Was there a significance in the fact that Charles held the baby before handing him to his mother? It was tempting to think so – one future king in the arms of another.

Charles chose his grandmother's 82nd birthday for William's christening. Four generations (below left) had much to smile about, though eventually William became just too hungry (below right). Six months later, William stayed at a farmstead in Australia while his parents toured the country (opposite) on their first, and highly successful, Royal Tour together. Charles mentioned his son in almost every official speech.

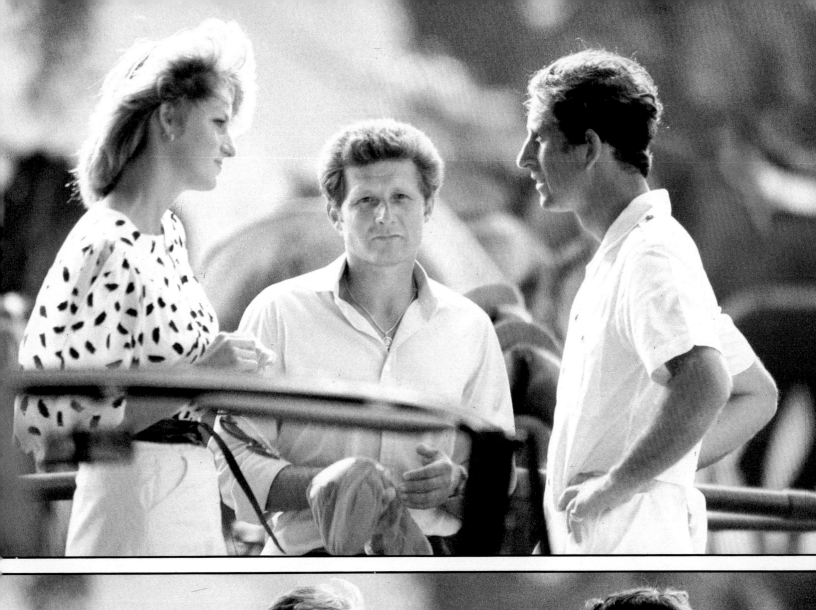

(Previous pages) informality at home and abroad: Charles and Diana both explore the lower slopes of Ayers Rock at the beginning of their tour of Australia in March 1983 and, back home that summer, they enjoy an afternoon out at Windsor. The eight weeks of tours, which, in the first half of 1983, took them to Australia, New Zealand and Canada (these pages), gave Charles the opportunity to show his wife places she had never visited before, and people she could only have read about – like the Aborigines at Ayers Rock (centre left) and the Maoris at Auckland (bottom right).

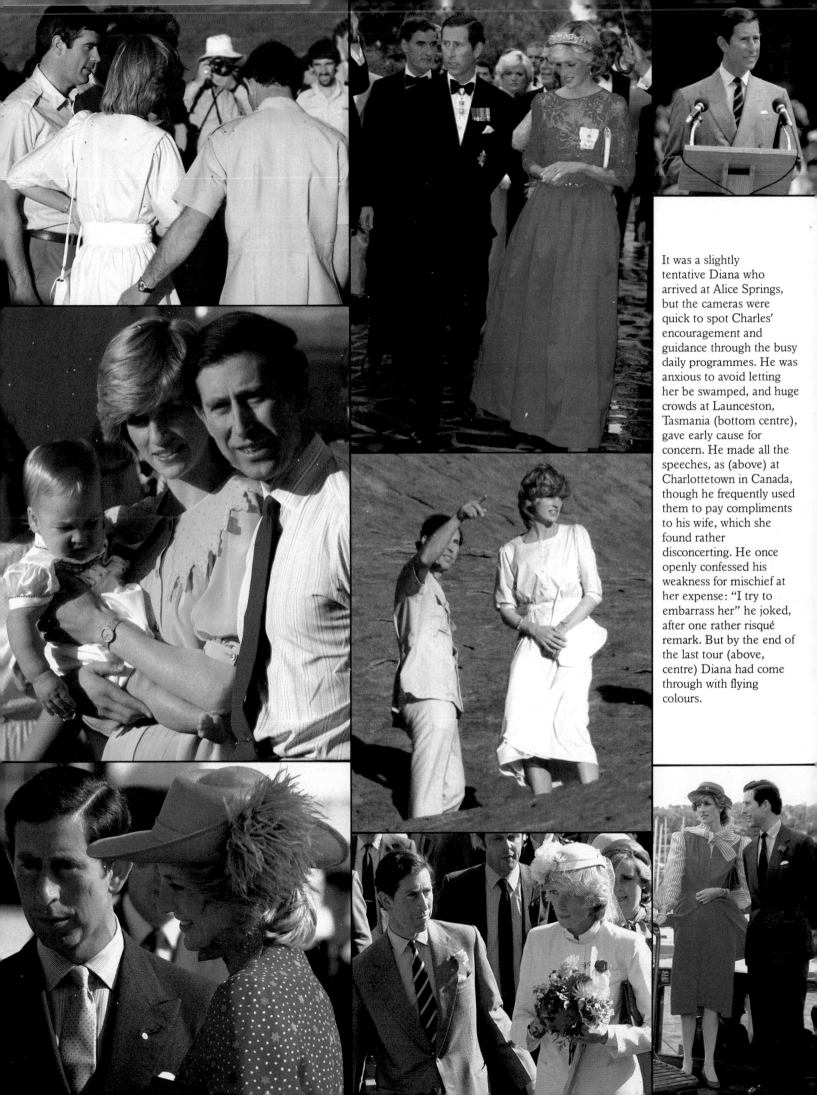

It was a slightly tentative Diana who arrived at Alice Springs, but the cameras were quick to spot Charles' encouragement and guidance through the busy daily programmes. He was anxious to avoid letting her be swamped, and huge crowds at Launceston, Tasmania (bottom centre), gave early cause for concern. He made all the speeches, as (above) at Charlottetown in Canada, though he frequently used them to pay compliments to his wife, which she found rather disconcerting. He once openly confessed his weakness for mischief at her expense: "I try to embarrass her" he joked, after one rather risqué remark. But by the end of the last tour (above, centre) Diana had come through with flying colours.

Charles was faintly amused by the sound of everyone demanding to see Diana. "I am afraid you'll have to make do with me", was his frequent response when people on both sides of the road wanted to see his wife. "It would have been easier to have two wives", he said later, in New Zealand. But he did at least bring Prince William, and the knowledge that the nine-month- old baby was among them melted many hearts down under. These pictures of young William, clearly at home in the Australian climate and (overleaf) having fun on the lawn of Government House in Auckland, meant a lot to admirers who only four months previously could never have suspected that he would make such an early round-the-world trip. Back home, Charles often takes his turn to carry William on and off aircraft (left).

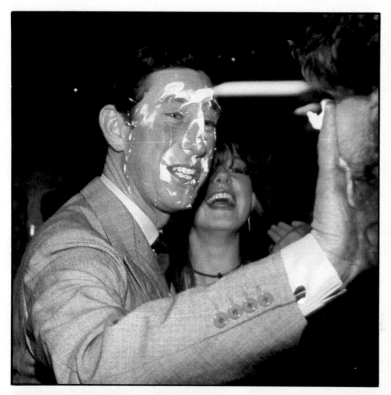

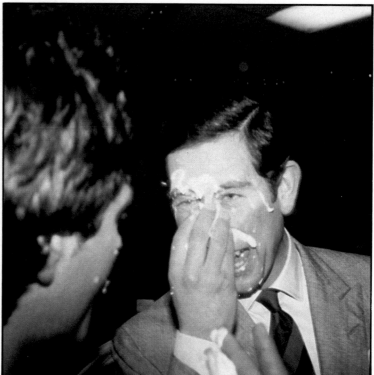

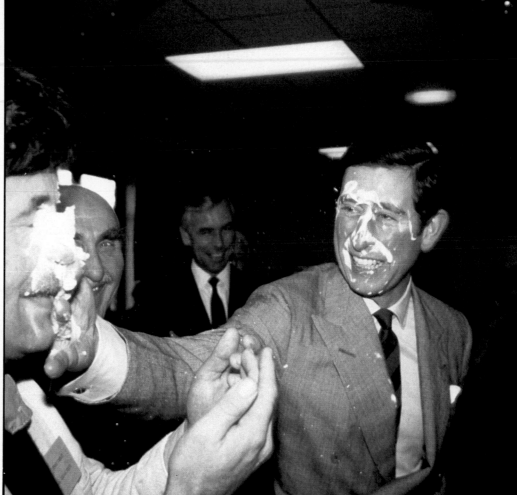

Custard-pie fun for Prince Charles during his visit to a West Indian community centre in Manchester in December 1983. It wasn't the first time he had been on the receiving end of slapstick comedy: the same thing happened during his brief amateur acting career at Cambridge in 1969, when he took part in a university production of Joe Orton's *Erpingham Camp*.

Although domestic details about the Royal Family are not normally discussed publicly, Charles agreed to talk about his family during the broadcast from Alice Springs (bottom left) to children in the Australian Outback. Diana answered a few questions as well, though rather nervously so that Charles felt obliged to prompt her. But he was clearly proud of his wife's superb dress sense, which brought endless remarks everywhere – nowhere more than at Melbourne (top left), on their last night in Australia. They were almost always together, from Masterton (above right) to Waitangi (opposite page, top left), and from Hobart (right) to Sydney (opposite page, bottom left).

The varied lifestyle of the Prince: as Doctor of Laws at Alberta University (top right); as spectator in the rain at Halifax (above); as welcome guest of the Maoris (right); as proud husband in Ottawa (below right); and as appreciative audience in Auckland (below). (Overleaf) Charles takes a back seat as Diana shimmers in sparkling silver at a Melbourne dinner-dance, and in a smooth silk off-the-shoulder lilac gown at a ballet gala in Auckland.

Amid all the formality, Prince Charles took his wife to Wanganui Collegiate, while in New Zealand, to meet Prince Edward (above). Even though the brothers had not seen each other for seven months, Charles' first remark poked fun at the kiwi-feathered cloak his brother Prince Edward was wearing. "My God", he said, "it must be a fancy-dress party. What have you come as?" Two months later it was Charles who wore the fancy dress (right and above left) as he accompanied Diana to a Klondike-style entertainment at Fort Edmonton. The outfit was almost identical to the one worn by Edward VII during his North American visit in 1860.

Prince Charles is renowned for injecting humour and informality into his public duties wherever possible. At Hobart (top) he joked about Tasmania's wedding present which "ensured that our son was born with at least six silver spoons in his mouth". He ribbed the Canadians for the poor weather in Halifax (left), and kept the republican-minded Australian premier smiling during the visit to Canberra (far left). A few private words with Diana – at a Sydney dance (above) or at the St John's Day celebrations (top left) – made unexpected pictures, as did their sudden decision to mingle with crowds after a Royal Albert Hall concert one January night (centre left).

(These pages) Prince Charles in his typical, sunny mood. By expansive smiles, as on arrival at Alice Springs (above) or at St Andrews in Canada (right), and by the spontaneous wave of the hand, as at Shelburne (left), he knows how easy it is to reward the patience and loyalty of crowds for whom the opportunity to see him may occur only once in a lifetime.

Charles regards the right to enjoy a leisurely holiday now and again as sacrosanct. After a ski-ing trip to Liechtenstein in 1983 was spoiled by the world's Press, he approved a properly-arranged photo-session in exchange for a promise to be left alone for the 1984 holiday. The result was some excellent pictures, such as those overleaf, and a few days' much-needed peace and quiet for the royal couple.